P9-DHP-086

# The United States Postal Service

*Neither snow nor rain nor heat nor gloom of night*
*stays these couriers*
*from the swift completion of their appointed rounds.*

KNOW YOUR GOVERNMENT

# The United States Postal Service

## Cheryl Weant McAfee

EAST CHICAGO PUBLIC LIBRARY
EAST CHICAGO, INDIANA

CHELSEA HOUSE PUBLISHERS
New York • New Haven • Philadelphia

ML /82 9003

Copyright © 1987 by Chelsea House Publishers, 5014 West Chester Pike,
Edgemont, Pa. 19028. All rights reserved.
  Reproduction in whole or part by any means whatsoever
  without permission of the publisher is prohibited by law.
Printed in the United States of America.

KG3-001087

**Library of Congress Cataloging-in-Publication Data**

McAfee, Cheryl Weant.
  United States Postal Service.
  (Know your government)
  Bibliography: p. 89
  Includes index.
  1. Postal Service—United States—History.
I. Title. II. Series: Know your government
(New York, N.Y.)
HE6371.M35 1987 353.0087'3 86-21556

ISBN 0-87754-826-9

Project Editor: Nancy Priff
Book Editor: Rafaela Ellis
Art Director: Maureen McCafferty
Series Designer: Anita Noble
Chief Copy Editor: Melissa R. Padovani
Project Coordinator: Kathleen P. Luczak
Production Manager: Brian A. Shulik

**ABOUT THE COVER**

The train, truck, and airplane represent transportation advances that have
helped the United States Postal Service (USPS) grow. Today, the eagle on the
USPS seal reflects the agency's growth in speed and efficiency. This seal
replaces the original one (shown on page 2), which depicted a mail carrier on
horseback.

YA
383.49
M113u

# CONTENTS

# KNOW YOUR GOVERNMENT

Titles in this series include:

# INTRODUCTION

# Government: Crises of Confidence

## Arthur M. Schlesinger, jr.

From the start, Americans have regarded their government with a mixture of reliance and mistrust. The men who founded the republic did not doubt the indispensability of government. "If men were angels," observed the 51st Federalist Paper, "no government would be necessary." But men are not angels. Since human beings are subject to wicked as well as to noble impulses, government was deemed essential to assure freedom and order.

At the same time, the American revolutionaries knew that government could also become a source of injury and oppression. The men who gathered in Philadelphia in 1787 to write the Constitution therefore had two purposes in mind. They wanted to establish a strong central authority and to limit that central authority's capacity to abuse its power.

To prevent the abuse of power, the founding fathers wrote two basic principles into the new Constitution. The principle of federalism divided power between the state governments and the central authority. The principle of the separation of powers subdivided the central authority itself into three branches—the executive, the legislative, and the judiciary—so that "each may be a check on the other." The *Know Your Government* series focuses on the major executive departments and agencies in these branches of the federal government.

The Constitution did not plan the executive branch in any detail. After vesting the executive power in the president, it assumed the existence of "executive departments" without specifying what these departments should be. Congress began defining their functions in 1789 by creating the Departments of State, Treasury, and War. The secretaries in charge of these departments made up President Washington's first cabinet. Congress also provided for a legal officer, and President Washington soon invited the attorney general, as he was called, to attend cabinet meetings. As need required, Congress created more executive departments.

Setting up the cabinet was only the first step in organizing the American state. With almost no guidance from the Constitution, President Washington, seconded by Alexander Hamilton, his brilliant secretary of the treasury, equipped the infant republic with a working administrative structure. The Federalists believed in both executive energy and executive accountability and set high standards for public appointments. The Jeffersonian opposition had less faith in strong government and preferred local government to the central authority. But when Jefferson himself became president in 1801, although he set out to change the direction of policy, he found no reason to alter the framework the Federalists had erected.

By 1801 there were about 3,000 federal civilian employees in a nation of a little more than 5 million people. Growth in territory and population steadily enlarged national responsibilities. Thirty years later, when Jackson was president, there were more than 11,000 government workers in a nation of 13 million.

The federal establishment was increasing at a faster rate than the population.

Jackson's presidency brought significant changes in the federal service. He believed that the executive branch contained too many officials who saw their jobs as "species of property" and as "a means of promoting individual interest." Against the idea of a permanent service based on life tenure, Jackson argued for the periodic redistribution of federal offices, contending that this was the democratic way and that official duties could be made "so plain and simple that men of intelligence may readily qualify themselves for their performance." He called this policy rotation-in-office. His opponents called it the spoils system.

In fact, partisan legend exaggerated the extent of Jackson's removals. More than 80 percent of federal officeholders retained their jobs. Jackson discharged no larger a proportion of government workers than Jefferson had done a generation earlier. But the rise in these years of mass political parties gave federal patronage new importance as a means of building the party and of rewarding activists. Jackson's successors were less restrained in the distribution of spoils. As the federal establishment grew—to nearly 40,000 by 1861—the politicization of the public service excited increasing concern.

After the Civil War the spoils system became a major political issue. High-minded men condemned it as the root of all political evil. The spoilsmen, said the British commentator James Bryce, "have distorted and depraved the mechanism of politics." Patronage, by giving jobs to unqualified, incompetent, and dishonest persons, lowered the standards of public service and nourished corrupt political machines. Office-seekers pursued presidents and cabinet secretaries without mercy. "Patronage," said Ulysses S. Grant after his presidency, "is the bane of the presidential office." "Every time I appoint someone to office," said another political leader, "I make a hundred enemies and one ingrate." George William Curtis, the president of the National Civil Service Reform League, summed up the indictment. He said,

> The theory which perverts public trusts into party spoils, making public employment dependent upon personal favor and not on proved merit, necessarily ruins the self-respect of public employees, destroys the function of party in a republic, prostitutes elections into a desperate strife for personal profit, and degrades the national character by lowering the moral tone and standard of the country.

The object of civil service reform was to promote efficiency and honesty in the public service and to bring about the ethical regeneration of public life. Over bitter opposition from politicians, the reformers in 1883 passed the Pendleton Act, establishing a bipartisan Civil Service Commission, competitive examinations, and appointment on merit. The Pendleton Act also gave the president authority to extend by executive order the number of "classified" jobs—that is, jobs subject to the merit system. The act applied initially only to about 14,000 of the more than 100,000 federal positions. But by the end of the 19th century 40 percent of federal jobs had moved into the classified category.

Civil service reform was in part a response to the growing complexity of American life. As society grew more organized and problems more technical, official duties were no longer so plain and simple that any person of intelligence could perform them. In public service, as in other areas, the all-round man was yielding ground to the expert, the amateur to the professional. The excesses of the spoils system thus provoked the counter-ideal of scientific public administration, separate from politics and, as far as possible, insulated against it.

The cult of the expert, however, had its own excesses. The idea that administration could be divorced from policy was an illusion. And in the realm of policy, the expert, however much segregated from partisan politics, can never attain perfect objectivity. He remains the prisoner of his own set of values. It is these values rather than technical expertise that determine fundamental judgments of public policy. To turn over such judgments to experts, moreover, would be to abandon democracy itself; for in a democracy final decisions must be made by the people and their elected representatives. "The business of the expert," the British political scientist Harold Laski rightly said, "is to be on tap and not on top."

Politics, however, were deeply ingrained in American folkways. This meant intermittent tension between the presidential government, elected every four years by the people, and the permanent government, which saw presidents come and go while it went on forever. Sometimes the permanent government knew better than its political masters; sometimes it opposed or sabotaged valuable new initiatives. In the end a strong president with effective cabinet secretaries could make the permanent government responsive to presidential purpose, but it was often an exasperating struggle.

The struggle within the executive branch was less important, however, than the growing impatience with bureaucracy in society as a whole. The 20th century saw a considerable expansion of the federal establishment. The Great Depression and the New Deal led the national government to take on a variety of new responsibilities. The New Deal extended the federal regulatory apparatus. By 1940, in a nation of 130 million people, the number of federal workers for the first time passed the 1 million mark. The Second World War brought federal civilian employment to 3.8 million in 1945. With peace, the federal establishment declined to around 2 million by 1950. Then growth resumed, reaching 2.8 million by the 1980s.

The New Deal years saw rising criticism of "big government" and "bureaucracy." Businessmen resented federal regulation. Conservatives worried about the impact of paternalistic government on individual self-reliance, on community responsibility, and on economic and personal freedom. The nation in effect renewed the old debate between Hamilton and Jefferson in the early republic, although with an ironic exchange of positions. For the Hamiltonian constituency, the "rich and well-born," once the advocate of affirmative government, now condemned government intervention, while the Jeffersonian constituency, the plain people, once the advocate of a weak central government and of states' rights, now favored government intervention.

In the 1980s, with the presidency of Ronald Reagan, the debate has burst out with unusual intensity. According to conservatives, government intervention abridges liberty, stifles enterprise, and is inefficient, wasteful, and arbitrary. It disturbs the harmony of the self-adjusting market and creates worse troubles than it solves. Get government off our backs, according to the popular cliché, and our problems will solve themselves. When government is necessary, let it be at the local level, close to the people. Above all, stop the inexorable growth of the federal government.

In fact, for all the talk about the "swollen" and "bloated" bureaucracy, the federal establishment has not been growing as inexorably as many Americans seem to believe. In 1949, it consisted of 2.1 million people. Thirty years later, while the country had grown by 70 million, the federal force had grown only by 750,000. Federal workers were a smaller percentage of the population in 1985 than they were in 1955—or in 1940. The federal establishment, in short, has not kept pace with population growth. Moreover, national defense and the postal service account for 60 percent of federal employment.

Why then the widespread idea about the remorseless growth of government? It is partly because in the 1960s the national government assumed new and intrusive functions:

12

affirmative action in civil rights, environmental protection, safety and health in the workplace, community organization, legal aid to the poor. Although this enlargement of the federal regulatory role was accompanied by marked growth in the size of government on all levels, the expansion has taken place primarily in state and local government. Whereas the federal force increased by only 27 percent in the 30 years after 1950, the state and local government force increased by an astonishing 212 percent.

Despite the statistics, the conviction flourishes in some minds that the national government is a steadily growing behemoth swallowing up the liberties of the people. The foes of Washington prefer local government, feeling it is closer to the people and therefore allegedly more responsive to popular needs. Obviously there is a great deal to be said for settling local questions locally. But local government is characteristically the government of the locally powerful. Historically, the way the locally powerless have won their human and constitutional rights has often been through appeal to the national government. The national government has vindicated racial justice against local bigotry, defended the Bill of Rights against local vigilantism, and protected natural resources against local greed. It has civilized industry and secured the rights of labor organizations. Had the states' rights creed prevailed, there would perhaps still be slavery in the United States.

The national authority, far from diminishing the individual, has given most Americans more personal dignity and liberty than ever before. The individual freedoms destroyed by the increase in national authority have been in the main the freedom to deny black Americans their rights as citizens; the freedom to put small children to work in mills and immigrants in sweatshops; the freedom to pay starvation wages, require barbarous working hours, and permit squalid working conditions; the freedom to deceive in the sale of goods and securities; the freedom to pollute the environment—all freedoms that, one supposes, a civilized nation can readily do without.

"Statements are made," said President John F. Kennedy in 1963, "labelling the Federal Government an outsider, an intruder, an adversary. . . . The United States Government is not a stranger or not an enemy. It is the people of fifty states joining in a national effort. . . . Only a great national effort by a great people working together can explore the mysteries of space, harvest the products at the bottom of the ocean, and mobilize the human, natural, and material resources of our lands."

So an old debate continues. However, Americans are of two minds. When pollsters ask large, spacious questions—Do you think government has become too involved in your lives? Do you think government should stop regulating business?—a sizable majority opposes big government. But when asked specific questions about the practical work of government—Do you favor social security? unemployment compensation? Medicare? health and safety standards in factories? environmental protection? government guarantee of jobs for everyone seeking employment? price and wage controls when inflation threatens?—a sizable majority approves of intervention.

In general, Americans do not want less government. What they want is more efficient government. They want government to do a better job. For a time in the 1970s, with Vietnam and Watergate, Americans lost confidence in the national government. In 1964, more than three-quarters of those polled had thought the national government could be trusted to do right most of the time. By 1980 only one-quarter was prepared to offer such trust. But by 1984 trust in the federal government to manage national affairs had climbed back to 45 percent.

Bureaucracy is a term of abuse. But it is impossible to run any large organization, whether public or private, without a bureaucracy's division of labor and hierarchy of authority. And

14

we live in a world of large organizations. Without bureaucracy modern society would collapse. The problem is not to abolish bureaucracy, but to make it flexible, efficient, and capable of innovation.

Two hundred years after the drafting of the Constitution, Americans still regard government with a mixture of reliance and mistrust—a good combination. Mistrust is the best way to keep government reliable. Informed criticism is the means of correcting governmental inefficiency, incompetence, and arbitrariness; that is, of best enabling government to play its essential role. For without government, we cannot attain the goals of the founding fathers. Without an understanding of government, we cannot have the informed criticism that makes government do the job right. It is the duty of every American citizen to *Know Your Government*—which is what this series is all about.

*Today, postal service reaches almost every American, and mailboxes line even the remotest stretches of the landscape.*

# ONE

# Communications and the Postal Service

The oldest organization in the federal government, the postal service has helped the country communicate for more than 275 years. It moves the mails and provides many other services for almost every American nearly every day. But communication hasn't always been easy and neither has the job of the postal service. Although it may be hard to imagine a time when writing or delivering a letter was difficult, the colonists and postal servants in the early 1700s often found these seemingly simple acts to be difficult and tedious.

First of all, many colonists couldn't read and write. Even if a colonist was literate, he'd have to get the proper writing supplies—paper, ink, and quill pens. Paper and ink were expensive because they had to be imported. Quill pens had to be made from clean turkey or goose feathers and were difficult to write with. Next, the colonist would have to write the letter. A short one would be best, because a two- or three-page letter would double or triple the cost.

Many of these things caused problems for the postal workers, too. They had to decipher addresses written by barely literate colonists whose quill pens often left smears and blotches on the paper. And because postal charges for a letter were based on the number of pages it contained and the distance it had to travel, postage calculations were difficult, too.

Because home pickup and delivery weren't available, the colonists had to walk to the local tavern to post and receive their mail. And of course, they couldn't expect a swift reply. Letters could take months—or even years—to reach their destination.

Today, the United States Postal Service (USPS) efficiently handles about 140 billion pieces of mail each year, delivering many of them to their destinations overnight. Although its status has changed from that of a federal agency to that of an independent government corporation, the USPS continues to serve the entire nation. It not only offers a wide range of delivery services for everything from letters to parcels and magazines but also

*America's first postal service operated out of local taverns, where citizens could post and retrieve their mail.*

*Huge trucks are only part of the USPS's fleet of vehicles.*

provides customers with special services, such as the sale of postal insurance, the rental of post office boxes, and the overseas transmission of documents by satellite.

The amazing transformation from haphazard mail system to highly efficient postal organization took place over more than two centuries. In many ways, the growth of the postal service has paralleled the growth of the United States. As the country extended its borders westward, the postal service followed, providing service by pony express and other means to newly settled territories. When America joined the industrial revolution, the postal service got involved, too, using new modes of transportation and automated processing methods to speed mail service. Now, in the age of communication, this agency has become a vital part of the country's communication system—a system that touches the lives of all citizens. The USPS helps people keep in touch with family members, friends, businesses, service companies, and government agencies in the United States and in foreign countries as well.

*Benjamin Franklin's print shop became a post office in 1730.*

# TWO

# The Early Years

The earliest American settlers had no organized postal service. Although their small settlements dotted the coastline from New England to Florida, the settlers' religious, cultural, and political differences stirred up hostilities that inhibited communication. The lack of a standard currency stifled commerce and restricted relations between communities. For instance, settlers in New England tended to use furs instead of money, whereas settlers in Virginia used barrels of tobacco. So they couldn't always agree on the "price" of things. A further blow to colonial communication was the lack of good overland trails. Even where trails existed, they were often difficult or impossible to cross. People and goods moved between settlements mostly by means of vessels sailing up and down the coastline.

At first, most communication was between the settlers and their homelands, with only occasional letters sent to other settlements. Sometimes the colonists sent letters with friends who

*Britain's King William granted Neale a postal monopoly in the colonies.*

were traveling to the same destination. But usually they sent their letters with merchant ships. They could give them directly to the ship's captain or deposit them for pickup in sacks at designated taverns and coffeehouses. When the ship docked, people could claim any letters they received at specified taverns. The sender could pay for this service in advance, but the ship's captain usually had to wait to receive payment from the recipient of the letter.

Each colony developed its own postal service, which usually limited its range of letter delivery to the colony's boundaries. Some people tried to deliver mail regularly between the colonies, but no formal service existed until Thomas Neale organized one. Neale was a favorite of the royal family in England, where he served as master of the mint. In February of 1692, King William and Queen Mary granted him a 21-year patent to set up and maintain a post office in the colonies. The patent allowed him to keep all profits on this postal monopoly and didn't require him to show his account books for 20 years. Because Neale had no desire to visit the colonies, he appointed Andrew Hamilton, governor of the Jerseys, as his deputy postmaster.

Although most of the colonies supported Neale's postal system, Maryland and Virginia didn't approve of this monopoly on letter delivery. They did not want to lose the income from the postal service they operated within their borders. Many colonists avoided Neale's post by taking advantage of a loophole in the patent that allowed them to send private letters by independent messengers. Use of this alternative post severely reduced Neale's profits.

Besides this loss of revenue to independent messengers, Neale faced other serious problems. Lack of a standard currency forced him to accept different pay for the same services. In addition, poor roads and transportation made mail delivery inefficient. Eventually, Neale's efforts failed, and in 1699 he died bankrupt.

Neale's creditors, Andrew Hamilton and Robert West, continued to run the postal service until 1703, when Hamilton died. Hamilton's wife took over the postal monopoly until 1707, when the British crown bought back the patent and removed the postal

*Andrew Hamilton and his family controlled the colonial post for more than 20 years.*

system from private control. The crown then appointed John Hamilton, Andrew's son, as deputy postmaster general of the American branch of the British Post Office. In 1721, John Lloyd of Charleston, South Carolina, took over. Alexander Spotswood, former lieutenant governor of Virginia, assumed the position in 1730 and established a post office at Benjamin Franklin's print shop, in Philadelphia.

At that time, Franklin was a 31-year-old printer who was just beginning his postal and diplomatic careers. In 1753, after Head Lynch and Elliot Benger had served as postmasters general, Franklin was appointed joint deputy postmaster general along with William Hunter of Williamsburg, Virginia. When Hunter died in 1761, John Foxcroft of New York took over his position.

Until Franklin's appointment, the postal service had lost money consistently. Postal service under the crown was expensive, and the service was worse than that provided under the Neale patent. In addition, the colonists viewed postal rates as another form of taxation and tried to send letters without paying postage. As joint deputy postmaster general, Franklin improved the system. He traveled throughout the colonies, mapping better routes and improving schedules. Along with Hunter, Franklin set up special handling for newspapers, admitting all of them into the mails and letting them travel for free between printers. Franklin extended the postal routes to Canada and Florida and convinced the British to continue transatlantic service after skirmishes with France threatened to end it. He took great pride in the revenues collected from 1757 to 1760, because the colonial post had shown a profit for the first time.

Franklin's innovations, combined with greater communication between merchants and a growing number of literate people, helped increase the mail volume. However, problems still existed. Private carriers transported mail illegally, postal rates remained high, and roads and transportation were poor, especially in the South.

*Colonial newspaper printers were aided by special mailing rates instituted by Postmaster Benjamin Franklin.*

During the ten years before the American Revolution, the postal system declined as the colonists became increasingly unhappy with British rule. Because Franklin sympathized with his countrymen, the British crown branded him a troublemaker and dismissed him from office. The colonists were outraged at Franklin's dismissal, and hostilities toward the British increased. But the British post—under Foxcroft—continued to operate in the colonies.

Lack of satisfaction with the British post led William Goddard, a Baltimore newspaper publisher, to call for a "constitutional post office"—a colonial postal system separate from the British system. The northern colonies favored the plan and quickly signed up for post offices. Goddard appointed postmasters who contracted directly with postriders (horseback riders who carried mail between post offices). As hostilities with England increased, the number of rebel postmasters multiplied, until each major community was a link in Goddard's postal chain. By May of 1775, Goddard's postal service stretched from Ports-

*William Goddard established rebel post offices throughout the colonies.*

mouth, New Hampshire, to Williamsburg, Virginia. It was so successful that the British post lost money and Foxcroft was forced to dismiss its postriders.

In the same month, members of the Continental Congress met in Philadelphia and decided to create a new government. They knew that communication between the colonies would be crucial in maintaining a united front against the British, so they established an American post office on July 26, 1775. They appointed Franklin postmaster general at a salary of $1,000 a year. Franklin appointed his son-in-law, Richard Bache, to manage finances. William Goddard also worked for the new American post office. He traveled throughout the colonies as its surveyor—the forerunner of today's postal inspector. In this position, he set up post offices, routes, and schedules; audited accounts; and investigated thefts.

The most important function of the first American postal service was to ensure speedy communication between Congress and the armies. During the war, the post office supplemented its normal service in two ways. It hired special couriers to carry congressional messages over the route between Cambridge, Massachusetts, and Philadelphia. It also added advice boats, which traveled along the coast delivering messages between Congress and the armies in the South. Although mail service to the public suffered, congressional communications to the armies flowed fairly smoothly.

After the war, the post office grew with the new nation. As people started to settle in the western territories, the new post-master general, Ebenezer Hazard, expanded postal service to the new settlements. At Hazard's suggestion, Congress codified the laws and regulations of the post office in 1782. This act set up the postal system as a federal government monopoly, which

*As settlers moved west, so did postal service.*

meant that only the postmaster general or his deputies could deliver letter mail. It formally established the system that would serve routes within and between states. It also limited postal rates to the amount needed to cover costs. And if the post office made a profit, the law required that these profits be used to pay any debts to the Treasury and to improve the postal system.

After the revolutionary war, the young nation's leaders focused on creating a new government. At the time, the post office was the only government system firmly in place—Franklin had built a solid foundation for it and later postmaster generals had strengthened it. The leaders were happy with its operation and had more pressing issues to resolve. So they agreed on a temporary act to sustain the postal service while they concentrated on creating the rest of the government. After much debate, Congress ratified the Constitution in March of 1789. The new president, George Washington, appointed Samuel Osgood of

*Samuel Osgood served as postmaster under George Washington.*

*When the federal government relocated to Washington, D.C., in 1800, this building became post office headquarters.*

Massachusetts as postmaster general. When Osgood stepped into the position, the postal system consisted of 75 post offices, 1,875 miles (3,024 kilometers) of post road, and 18 contracts with postriders for carrying the mail.

Throughout these early years, the post office was part of the Treasury Department. In 1790 and 1791, Congress again passed temporary laws to continue the postal service. As the nation grew, mail volume increased dramatically. In 1800, when the federal government moved its headquarters from Philadelphia to Washington, D.C., the burgeoning post office was the first to depart.

As the post office expanded, it gained power. During Andrew Jackson's presidency, William T. Barry of Kentucky joined the president's cabinet as postmaster general. On June 8, 1872, Congress officially established the Post Office Department as an executive department.

For many years, private companies carried letters like these across the country.

# THREE

# Development of the Postal Service

$\mathbf{F}$our major factors influenced the growth and development of the Post Office Department: changes in transportation, development and improvement of postal services, innovations in automation, and the expense of operating the department (which led the government to reorganize it and convert it from a regular agency to an independent corporation).

## Transportation

In many ways, the growth of the post office in the 18th, 19th, and 20th centuries has reflected changes in transportation. Since the early days of the postal service, people have searched for faster and more efficient ways to transport the mail. As people began to move farther from established communities, the post office had to increase its search for new forms of transportation to deliver the mail.

As the country expanded westward, people moved to the Louisiana, Oregon, and California territories. Despite conflicts with Indians, hunger, disease, and many other hardships, pioneer families searched for new and better lives in the West. The mail had to follow these settlers to encourage and support commerce, to bring news of families and friends, and most important, to help ensure a united nation. Particularly in the late 1700s and early 1800s, government officials were worried that the people in the emerging western settlements would be easy prey for other governments and individuals who wanted to disrupt the nation or claim territory as their own. So as early as 1782, Ebenezer Hazard concentrated on improving inland postal service. He wanted to make sure that the isolated communities received personal mail as well as newspapers and announcements containing government information.

To keep these lines of communication open, the post office needed brave riders and strong horses. It also needed new and improved trails and roads through the vast expanses of wilderness. Sometimes riders were forced to cross bridgeless streams on horseback or swim across flood-swollen creeks while holding their mailbags aloft. But no matter what hardships and dangers the postriders faced, they still had to deliver the mail and deliver it on schedule. In 1810, one heroic postrider, Samuel Lewis, managed to deliver the mail even though he had been struck on the head by a log while searching a flooded stream for his mailbag. He was, however, a few days late.

Many settlements were accessible only by boat. As early as 1813, the postmaster general authorized contracts for steamboat service between New Orleans, Louisiana, and Natchez, Mississippi. By 1823 steamboats had become such a common form of mail transport that Congress passed an act declaring all steamboat routes to be "post roads."

As people settled farther west, mail was also transported by the army, contract postriders, and private express carriers (pri-

**Steamboats transported mail to hard-to-reach areas.**

vate companies that provided faster mail service for a fee). One famous mail carrier was Kit Carson. While working for the army in 1848, he carried the first overland mail from coast to coast.

At the same time, transport by ship was another important form of coast-to-coast mail service. This service required three contracts: one moved the mail from New York to Panama by ship, the second moved it across the narrow Isthmus of Panama by rail, and the third moved it to San Francisco by ship. The *California* was the first westbound steamship to carry mail from Panama. It reached San Francisco in 1848. However, its return trip was greatly delayed because the ship's crew deserted to look for gold, which had just been discovered nearby.

Problems with steamship service led to the founding of a transcontinental land route from St. Louis to San Francisco. The post office awarded John Butterfield a six-year contract to transport mail on this route by stagecoach in semiweekly trips. His Overland Mail Company was successful, even though it often missed its 24-day schedule for mail delivery. By 1860, it was carrying more letter mail than the steamships.

At about the same time, private express carriers such as William H. Russell saw the westward expansion as an opportunity

*The Overland Mail Company's stagecoaches carried mail from St. Louis to San Francisco.*

to make money. Russell was a transportation entrepreneur who had some mail delivery contracts with the post office. Because the railroad and telegraph went only as far west as St. Joseph, Missouri, he wanted another contract with the post office to run a year-round express mail service between St. Joseph and San Francisco. However, the Senate Post Office and Post Road Committee did not support his idea.

Undaunted, Russell decided to launch his own business—the pony express—which became the best known of all private express services. He and his partners prepared relay stations, bought hearty horses that could withstand the elements, and hired riders. Although rough terrain, terrible weather, and warring Indians threatened to make the job dangerous, Russell recruited a staff of express riders.

On April 3, 1860, the first run of the pony express began. Its first rider, Billy Richardson, took the central route through Missouri, Kansas, Nebraska, Colorado, Wyoming, Utah, Nevada, and California. Like subsequent riders, Richardson had to complete his route in ten-and-one-half days. To do this, he had to transfer his mochila (a leather saddle cover with a small, locked mail pouch) to a fresh horse, which he had to mount in 2 minutes, at relay stations spaced about 15 miles (24 kilometers) apart.

Winter weather slowed the pony express's mail run to 15 days, and Indian attacks interrupted service in May and June of 1860. But Russell and his partners continued to operate the pony express until July 1, 1861, when the Post Office Department contracted to operate it. On October 26, 1861, the pony express passed into legend when the transcontinental telegraph was completed.

Although the railroad had been around for more than 30 years before the pony express, it didn't reach its full potential for mail transport until the 1860s. As early as 1832, the Post Office

*Pony express riders braved bad weather and Indian attacks.*

Department had officially recognized the railroad as a viable means of transporting mail. In that year, it granted a yearly railroad allowance of $400 to contractors who had previously moved the mail from Philadelphia to Lancaster, Pennsylvania, by stage. This money allowed them to carry the mail by train for part of the route, from Philadelphia to West Chester, a distance of 30 miles (48 kilometers).

After that time, the railroads gained support as a means of mail transport. On July 7, 1838, Congress passed an act making all railroad lines post roads. In the 1840s the availability of locomotive headlights made night travel possible, and in the 1850s the number of lighted cars greatly increased. Throughout the 1850s and 1860s, the use of the telegraph to control rail traffic enabled the railroads to improve their safety and schedules, which in turn improved the mail service.

GREAT U. S. MAIL AND EXPRESS ROUTE.

MORTH MISSOURI

RAIL  ROAD

THE ONLY RAIL ROAD ROUTE FROM

ST. LOUIS TO ST. JOSEPH.

THROUGH IN 17 HOURS.

THE ONLY DIRECT ROUTE TO

CINCINNATI, LOUISVILLE, LEXINGTON, BALTIMORE,

Washington, Philadelphia, and all points East and South.

Tickets for sale at all Ticket Offices of Hannibal & St. Joseph Rail Road. Be particular to get your Tickets via North Missouri Railroad.

W. B. MOULTON. Superintendent.

WILLIAM MORIN, Agent, St. Joseph.

*By the mid-1800s, passenger trains included mail in their cargo when they traveled to the western states.*

*Postal clerks sorted
mail in transit
aboard railway post
offices.*

During the 1840s, mail clerks traveled on the trains with the mail that came from large post offices. They sorted mail for delivery along their railroad line, but not for connecting lines or routes beyond their destinations. William A. Davis, an assistant postmaster at St. Joseph, Missouri, helped change that. In July of 1862, Davis was the first clerk to sort mail officially for connecting routes while the train was underway. The success of Davis's experiment supported the idea of traveling post offices, which George B. Armstrong had developed in 1854. So Armstrong, the assistant postmaster of Chicago, submitted detailed plans to postal officials in Washington for railway post offices (RPOs)— special railroad cars outfitted for mail sorting. He explained how postal clerks aboard the RPOs would sort all mail for advance connections and local exchanges. He also pointed out that RPO service would not interrupt letter transit and would reduce the amount of sorting that clerks had to do at terminals. Postal officials approved his idea.

On August 28, 1864, the post office put the first RPO into operation on the Chicago and North Western Railroad between Chicago and Clinton, Iowa. The new service had its own employ-

*Railway post offices used devices to fling mailbags into trackside mail catchers as the train moved.*

ees who worked in specially constructed, 40-foot (12-meter) RPO cars. They delivered mail "on the fly": as the train slowed down, an agent on the train handed the mailbag to an agent on the platform. To make this task less hazardous, the post office soon developed a trackside mail catcher. Although the RPOs were originally designed for letter mail only, they soon handled newspaper mail as well. Railroad mail delivery became so successful that it revolutionized the postal service and put an end to many steamboat and overland stage contracts.

Rail service and equipment continued to improve. In addition to better construction, heating, lighting, and signaling in railcars, Fast Mail trains made a dramatic improvement in mail service. Introduced in 1875, these trains ran between New York, Chicago, and St. Louis, and carried agents who processed mail in specially constructed RPO cars. Despite rail delivery's great success, the post office was forced to stop this service in 1876, when Congress cut back on railroad funding for carrying the

*Public demand brought back Fast Mail trains like this one.*

mail. The public was outraged and so were postal officials. By 1881 the post office was able to reinstitute Fast Mail train service.

In 1889 the post office inaugurated coast-to-coast Fast Mail service from New York to San Francisco. On the first run, the train was delayed by 38 minutes between Green River and Ogden, Utah. To make up the time, Engineer William "Wild Bill" Downing set a speed record and gave the officials on board such a harrowing ride that the general manager of the Union Pacific Railroad tried to stop the train.

Although the railroads provided excellent mail service to many cities and towns, rail lines did not extend into every area. So the post office experimented with other means of mail transport. For small villages that were not served by the railroad, the post office used wagons to move the mail. In 1877, the post office even developed standard designs for postal wagons—one of the first innovations in the street transport of mail.

Although at first they were used extensively, wagons had a limited future after the turn of the century. As early as 1895, the Post Office Department predicted that they would be replaced by "horseless wagons." This prediction was made four years before the creation of Henry Ford's first automobile company. As people began to use automobiles and trucks, wagon transport started to decline.

In some cities, the post office experimented with a method of transport based on RPOs, called the streetcar RPO system. In 1891, St. Louis Postmaster J.B. Harlowe arranged for mail collection and delivery by the electric and cable cars that passed through the city's streets. Postal and streetcar officials helped refine Harlowe's system. By 1895, postal employees pouched, canceled, and distributed mail on streetcars as part of the railway mail service. At its peak, the streetcar RPO system operated in 15 cities. Although the system was successful, the Post Office Department established few streetcar RPOs after 1900 because only the largest cities used them, and "horseless wagons" threatened to make them obsolete. The system ended in 1929 with the last run of the Baltimore streetcar RPO.

*Until automobiles made them obsolete, standardized mail wagons served small villages that rail lines missed.*

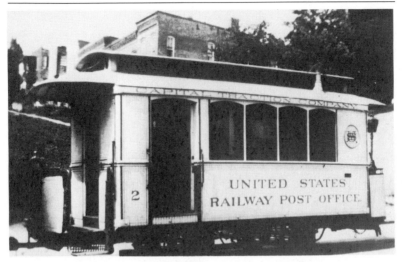

*Streetcar RPOs like the one above operated in more than a dozen cities until the service ceased in 1929.*

When automobiles and trucks became the preferred method of road transportation, the Post Office Department tried an experiment based on the streetcar RPOs. In 1941 it began to use specially built motor vehicles called Highway Post Offices (HPOs). Basically, the HPOs were large buses with interiors remodeled to resemble RPO cars, allowing mail sorting during transport. The HPOs traveled the highways for 24 years, supplementing rail service by carrying mail to areas that the trains couldn't reach. However, the post office phased out the HPOs when the decline of the railroads and advances in postal mechanization made in-transit processing obsolete.

During the late 1800s, the post office experimented with a little-known method of mail transport that could not be affected by bad weather—pneumatic tubes. Several European cities were already using this underground system of tubes through which compressed air propelled canisters of mail. In 1893 the Post Office Department tried its first pneumatic tube line in Philadelphia. Eventually it used pneumatic tube lines in six cities. Each

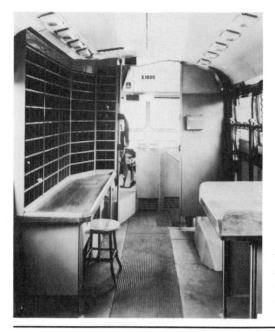

*Buses in the HPO system greatly resembled the RPOs they supplemented.*

21-inch- (53-centimeter-) long pneumatic canister held up to 600 letters and could move rapidly. During rush periods, the post office could move about 360,000 letters per hour. Clearly, the pneumatic tube system provided speedy delivery.

However, some believed that the system was too expensive. The Post Office Department leased the pneumatic tube equipment from private companies, and opponents of the system argued that the leasing costs were "exorbitant, unjustified, and an extravagant waste of public funds." In an effort to save money during World War I, the post office suspended pneumatic tube service in 1918, but the public clamored for its return. So the post office reinstituted the service in New York in 1922 and in Boston in 1926.

The pneumatic tube system began to decline during the Depression, when postal revenues dropped. Other problems also began to surface. Sometimes, small packages containing perfume, ball bearings, and other mobile objects would break open in the tubes and damage the other mail. At other times, jams would develop in the tubes, sometimes requiring workmen to creep along a 12-inch (30.5-centimeter) catwalk on a bridge to remove the blockage. When the post office officially suspended tube service on December 31, 1953, motor vehicles again transported intercity mail.

Of course, the post office had experimented with mail transport by motor vehicle much earlier. In 1899, it conducted its first experiments in Buffalo, New York, and Cleveland, Ohio. Postal officials found the Cleveland experiment particularly impressive. Despite a raging snowstorm and 22 miles (35 kilometers) of partially paved roads, the Winton motor truck delivered all the mail to the post office in 2 hours and 27 minutes—much faster than the 6 hours and 1 minute it took by horse-and-wagon delivery. Although the experiment was a success, the Post Office Department didn't issue contracts for truck service until October 1, 1906, in Baltimore.

*Postal clerks filled pneumatic canisters with mail for delivery to cities that used the system.*

*Automobiles slashed delivery time and transport costs.*

The Post Office Department began to purchase its own vehicles when the demand for this faster service increased and when it realized that some contractors were inflating their fees. By the end of 1918, it owned 1,004 vehicles. At first, it was haphazard about purchasing, garaging, and servicing its automobiles and trucks. But in 1921 the Post Office Department standardized its vehicles and supplies, opened maintenance garages, and created a management organization to oversee its auto and truck fleet. By 1984, it owned and operated 130,735 vehicles and employed 4,119 maintenance workers to keep them running smoothly.

Motor vehicle service was a boon to the Post Office Department, providing a link between post offices, railways, and households and making travel easier, cheaper, and more convenient. But the postal service's quest for fast, efficient delivery did not end there. In the early 20th century, it began to experiment with another method of transport—the airplane. With its daring pilots and fascinating flying machines, the early airmail service opened a glamorous chapter in postal history. But the airmail postal service did more than just carry mail successfully; it also laid the

44

groundwork for technical innovations that made today's air travel possible.

Unofficially, balloons, dirigibles, and airplanes had already been used occasionally to carry "airmail" in Europe and the United States. In 1911, Postmaster General Frank H. Hitchcock swore in pilot Earl Ovington as a mail carrier and gave him approval to carry United States mail from Garden City, New York, to Mineola, New York, during the International Aviation Tournament. Ovington didn't even have to land in Mineola; he simply had to drop the mailbags to the ground for the postmaster to pick up. On April 10, 1912, pilot George Mestach made the first regular United States mail flight between two cities. He completed the trip from New Orleans to Baton Rouge, Louisiana, in just 91 minutes.

After four years of petitioning Congress for money, the Post Office Department received $50,000 to fund its airmail service in 1916. However, the lack of suitable planes delayed the venture until 1918. At that time, the post office received $100,000 in new congressional funding and teamed up with the War Department

*Ovington (left) helped Hitchcock (center) inaugurate airmail.*

to launch an airmail service that used Army Signal Corps pilots and planes to fly the mail. Under this arrangement, student pilots got valuable training in cross-country flights, and the post office became able to transport its mail more rapidly.

On May 15, 1918, the new airmail service began officially on the New York-Philadelphia-Washington route. Planes were scheduled to take off from each of these cities. Despite the beautiful weather and a mood of excitement, the Washington pilot, Lt. George L. Boyle, must have thought the day was a disaster. With President Woodrow Wilson and other dignitaries looking on, Boyle slipped into the cockpit of his Curtiss biplane. In vain, he tried to start the engine, until a check revealed that the gas tank was almost empty. Embarrassed mechanics, who had not brought extra gas, quickly drained fuel from other planes and filled Boyle's tank. Relieved onlookers finally watched Boyle take off for Philadelphia, but instead of turning north, he headed south toward Richmond. Realizing his mistake, Boyle tried to land on a country road to ask directions. Instead, he brought the plane down in a plowed field in Maryland, breaking the plane's propeller. He was only 25 miles (40 kilometers) from his takeoff point. Nevertheless, the other pilots completed their trips and the experiment was considered a huge success.

For a few months, army pilots moved the mail in their Curtiss biplanes, affectionately known as "Jennies." Achieving an average speed of 72.56 miles (117.03 kilometers) per hour, they improved delivery time from Washington to New York by two to three hours over railway mail. Then on August 12, 1918, the Post Office Department took over all flight operations. It hired pilots and mechanics and purchased six specially designed mail planes from the Standard Aircraft Corporation. The government enthusiastically supported this expansion of the airmail service.

At first, airmail service had some major limitations. For instance, pilots could only fly in the daytime, because they needed to see ground landmarks to know where they were.

*A crowd cheered as mechanics started Boyle's biplane.*
*Although his flight ended in disaster, airmail was a success.*

(They usually used regular road maps to locate these land-marks.) Also, they had no instruments, radios, or runway lights to help guide them. So unexpected weather forced pilots to make many unplanned landings on unsuitable spots, such as farm fields and roads. Fortunately, the maneuverability and slow land-ing speed of these small planes helped limit the number of fatali-ties. And technological developments allowed the post office to improve and strengthen its mail planes and airfields. In August of 1920, it installed radio equipment at airfields to provide the pilots with timely weather reports and flight data.

The Post Office Department also improved its airmail ser-vice by adding a transcontinental route. To cover such a long distance, the post office planned a series of smaller routes, or legs. It opened the first two legs—from New York to Cleveland and from Cleveland to Chicago—in 1919. The third leg—from Chicago to Omaha—opened in 1920. Later that year, the final leg—from Omaha to San Francisco—opened, completing the transcontinental air route.

The first transcontinental flight took place on February 22 and 23, 1921. As two planes set out from San Francisco, two others left from New York. The eastbound flights proved to be particularly dramatic. In Reno, Nevada, one eastbound plane crashed, killing the pilot. At the Cheyenne-North Platte, Wyo-

*Jack Knight braved snow and fog during the first transcontinental air mail flight.*

ming, relay station, bonfires lining the landing field helped guide the other eastbound plane in for refueling. Pilot James H. "Jack" Knight took over the flight and soon encountered snow. When he landed at the Omaha field, which was lit only by burning gasoline drums, he found no relief pilot to fly the plane to Chicago. Although Knight was unfamiliar with that part of the route, he took off at 2 A.M. with a road map to help him locate landmarks.

At the Iowa City emergency field, Knight landed in a blizzard, guided by one colored flare that the night watchman had set out. After refueling, Knight took off into the blinding snow and began to search for Lake Michigan, his landmark for Chicago. When the snow finally ended, fog appeared. Almost miraculously, the fog cleared at daybreak, and Lake Michigan gleamed like a jewel in the morning sun. Jack Knight was a hero. The mail continued on to New York, completing the entire trip from San Francisco in 33 hours and 20 minutes. Despite the bad weather and the difficulties of night flying, the transcontinental air route was much faster than the 72-hour service by train.

Impressed with airmail's potential for better mail service,

Congress appropriated $1,250,000 to improve airfields and planes. The Post Office Department installed emergency landing fields, beacons, searchlights, towers, and boundary markers. It also improved planes by adding landing and navigational lights, lighted instrument panels, and parachute flares. Although night flying had only been a dream in 1920, it had become a reality in some areas of the country by 1923.

On February 2, 1925, Congress passed a law that encouraged commercial airlines to contract for airmail delivery. Response to this law eliminated the need for planes and pilots in the postal system. By 1927, the entire transcontinental route was under contract. The post office had transferred its radio service, lighted emergency runways, and beacons to the Department of Commerce. These measures gave commercial aviation a safe start and the benefit of the post office's innovations and improvements.

However, the limited space on airplanes and the small number of flights made airmail a premium service. Airmail rates were higher than rates for regular first-class mail, which was usually transported by train. These high rates restricted its use somewhat. But as commercial aviation expanded after World War II, so did airmail service. By the mid-1950s, regular first-class mail traveled by air whenever space was available, and the new jet aircraft moved the mail much faster. Eventually, airmail became so common that on May 1, 1977, the post office eliminated the separate service category and additional charge for airmail.

For many years, the Civil Aeronautics Board regulated all commercial airlines and required them to carry a certain amount of mail, based on weight, on each flight. The federal government passed the Airline Deregulation Act of 1978 to end the Civil Aeronautics Board, and in December of 1984, the board officially disbanded. Now the postal service contracts with individual airlines to carry mail, as it did in the 1920s and 1930s.

# Postal Service Improvements

Transportation improvements and innovations helped move the mail more quickly over great distances. Yet as the nation's population grew, the mail not only had to move faster—it had to move *better*. So the Post Office Department developed new services to make mail service more convenient for customers. It also began to use better and more efficient methods to handle, process, and deliver mail.

One of the most significant improvements was the change in postal rates and the method of rate payment. Before 1855, a person could choose to pay the postage when he sent a letter or he could let the addressee pay it when he picked up the letter. This was true even after the post office introduced postage stamps in 1847. However, the post office lost money whenever addressees refused to accept and pay for letters. So in 1855, Congress passed a law that abolished this method of payment for postage and required prepayment for all mail.

Until 1863, the post office didn't have a uniform postage rate, so it based the cost of mailing a letter on the number of pages and the distance traveled. For example, in 1792, an individual had to pay 6 cents to send a one-page letter 30 miles (48 kilometers). If he wanted to send the letter 450 miles (725 kilometers), he would have to pay 25 cents. And if he wanted to send a two- or three-page letter, he would have to pay double or triple that rate. Finally, in 1844, a statute established postal rates based on weight.

In 1863, the post office further refined its rates by classifying the mail into three groups: letters, regular printed matter, and other miscellaneous matter. Later that year, it regrouped mail into four classes: first, second, third, and fourth class. It also established a uniform rate of 3 cents per half-ounce. These rates were low in comparison to today's postal rates, mostly because the Treasury Department paid for all costs in excess of post

*One of America's first postage stamps featured George Washington's likeness.*

office revenues. It provided this subsidy until the Post Office Department was reorganized in 1971. Just before the reorganization, first-class stamps cost only 6 cents, and the Treasury financed 19.9 cents of every dollar of postal expenses. Now stamps cost nearly four times as much because the post office must cover all of its expenses without help from the Treasury.

In addition to improving the method of calculating postal rates, the post office refined its delivery techniques. Throughout the early years, most customers had to go to the post office to send or pick up mail. In large cities, customers could request home delivery, but they had to pay an extra fee. In the late 1850s, the Post Office Department improved its service throughout the East Coast by placing mail collection boxes on city streets. By 1863, it had also created free home delivery in 49 large cities, reducing the need for customers to travel to their local post offices. At first, home delivery was relatively slow, because mail carriers had to wait for each door to be answered to deliver the mail. Then, in 1878, the Post Office Department experimented with the idea of household letter boxes. These boxes made mail delivery much faster by eliminating the need for mail carriers to

*Public mailboxes improved collection services.*

wait at each door. However, the post office could not require all households to provide letter boxes until March 1, 1923, when the government passed a specific regulation.

When free delivery began in 1863, it did not include service to people in small towns, farm communities, or other rural areas that were isolated from large cities. Yet the post was many of these people's only link to the rest of the world. Rural residents had to travel into town to pick up their mail, and sometimes the distance was so long that they made their trips only once every two or three months.

To try to solve this problem, Congress appropriated funds in 1895 for an experiment in rural free delivery (RFD). In October of 1896, the test began with five carriers delivering mail to rural residents around post offices in Charles Town, Halltown, and Uvilla, West Virginia.

The inauguration of the RFD service received no fanfare. In fact, many politicians and voters opposed it. They claimed it was expensive and thought it was impractical because it required carriers to slog through muddy roads, climb over fences, and battle snowstorms simply to deliver the mail. However, rural residents strongly supported the service, and Congress appropriated funds for RFD expansion in 1898.

Soon after, rural residents flooded the post office with petitions to establish RFD routes in their areas. But the post office had to turn down many of them because of a lack of good roads. Anxious for RFD service, many farmers and other rural residents improved roads on their own. Between 1897 and 1908, state and local governments spent about $72,000,000 to repair existing roads and build new bridges and drains. In 1917, Congress passed the Federal Highway Act, which provided more money for road improvements. Although the post office didn't actually build the rural roads, its RFD service spurred their construction and improvement. And widespread road improvement eventually allowed the post office to provide extensive RFD service.

*As late as 1940, many RFD carriers traveled on horseback.*

RFD routes from large post offices served rural communities so well that the Post Office Department closed many small post offices and terminated many contract routes, eliminating many jobs. Because automobiles could handle longer routes than horses, rural route delivery by automobile threatened to eliminate even more jobs. To prevent further unemployment, Congress passed an act restricting the length of horse and automobile routes. At many post offices, one mail carrier would load his automobile while right next to him another packed his horse-drawn wagon to deliver the rural mail.

In the early 1900s, the needs of rural Americans prompted the Post Office Department to develop another important service—parcel post. Although country stores carried some provisions, rural residents had to order most of the goods they needed from large cities and have them shipped by private

*Horse-drawn wagons delivered mail on many RFD routes.*

express. The success of RFD routes encouraged rural dwellers to lobby for free parcel delivery by the post office. Of course, owners of private express companies and country stores opposed this because they thought it would lure away much of their business.

However, Congress passed a law in 1912 that created the parcel post; it began operation on January 1, 1913. This new postal service started a trend in mail-order advertising and sales. People found it easy and inexpensive to order from catalogs, and they liked the convenience of home delivery.

# Automation

As the number of new services and the population increased, so did the amount of mail the post office had to collect, postmark, cancel, sort, pouch, transport, and deliver. For years, postal clerks did each of these jobs by hand—a tedious and time-consuming process. They pigeonholed letters and canceled and postmarked stamps with hand stamps and ink pads, much the way clerks had done in Franklin's time.

In 1868, inventors began to patent stamp canceling machines. The post office experimented with these machines and, in 1876, bought one that had been invented by Thomas and Martin Leavitt of Boston. The purchase of this machine brought the post office into the mechanical age.

The Leavitt machine was operated with a hand crank and made stamp cancellation quicker and easier. In 1882, Congress adopted it as the standard. Then in 1884, the American Postal Machine Company introduced a belt-driven model that saved even more time and labor. By 1892, companies were developing machines that ran on electricity. The Post Office Department began renting machines and testing them until they were perfected. In the early 1900s, it also began to experiment with a conveyor system that carried mail automatically to each letter

*Innovations such as the cylinder postage meter cut hours from tedious postal work.*

carrier's sorting table. However, this form of conveyor system was unsuccessful because it proved impractical for sorting small amounts of mail.

To help process mail faster, the post office encouraged large-volume customers, such as businesses, to use precanceled stamps and special machines, including the automatic stamp affixing machine. In 1902, Arthur H. Pitney invented the meter machine, revolutionizing business mailings.

At the end of the 1800s, most post office buildings were not designed or equipped to handle the mail sorting process and the new automated equipment. So in 1910, Congress set aside special funds to improve the Post Office Department's buildings and equipment. This allowed the department to design new offices that could accommodate technical innovations. Because trains carried most of the mail, postal officials decided to construct new buildings close to railway stations. Then they authorized testing and installation of an improved conveyor system that moved large sacks of mail between train stations and post offices.

However, once the mail reached the post office, clerks still had to sort, stamp, and pouch it by hand. In the 1920s, the Post Office Department began testing machines that could perform what were then manual tasks. But the Depression and World War II slowed automation research until the 1950s, when the Post Office Department tested the first semiautomatic machine for parcel sorting in Baltimore. During this period, it also tested a letter-sorting machine and other specially designed equipment. By the 1960s and 1970s, improved letter-sorting and stamp-canceling machines had become the backbone of mail processing.

At about the same time, computer technology began to revolutionize mail service for consumers *and* the post office. Businesses used computers to centralize and process vast amounts of information for billing and advertising, increasing the volume of mail. To help route all of this mail properly, the Post Office Department introduced a code system, known as the Zone Improvement Plan (ZIP) code, on July 1, 1963. It assigned codes to addresses throughout the United States. The first digit represented one of ten large geographical areas. The second and third digits identified a metropolitan area, and the final two numbers denoted a small post office or local delivery area.

This new system required the establishment of large transportation centers nationwide to reduce the mail processing bur-

*Cartoon mailman Mr. Zip advertised the advantages of the ZIP code system.*

den on big city post offices. It also required further automation to handle ZIP coded mail efficiently. So in 1965, the Post Office Department introduced a machine that could sort by ZIP code—a high-speed optical character reader. To make mail processing even more efficient, the post office added four more digits to the ZIP code in 1983. These new digits are part of the ZIP + 4 code. They identify sectors, such as several blocks in an area, and segments, such as certain floors in large buildings.

In many large post offices, computer-driven optical character readers process mail with the new code. These machines read the address and print a bar code—similar to the pricing code on a can at the supermarket—on the envelope. When the envelope reaches its destination post office, a bar code sorter reads its bar code, just as a scanner reads pricing codes at a supermarket checkout. Then it sorts the letter into the proper holding area.

*Large post offices use optical character readers.*

*This illustration
shows how
INTELPOST beams
an image to a post
office on earth.*

New communications technologies have allowed the post office to experiment with providing different kinds of services. The International Electronic Post (INTELPOST) system transmits an image of a document by satellite to a post office that is specially equipped with a receiving device. Then a postal worker places the transmitted copy in an envelope for delivery by regular post. INTELPOST has served countries around the world since 1980.

# Departmental Reorganization

During the 1960s, tensions mounted between postal workers and managers. Postal officials and Congress realized that many problems existed in the Post Office Department. Although the department had moved its technology and management into the modern age, it still conducted much of its business the way it had 100 years before. Service deteriorated, and in 1966 the nation's largest postal facility, the 60-acre Chicago Post Office, ground to

*O'Brien
recommended
making the postal
service a
government
corporation.*

a halt for almost 2 weeks when the mail volume completely overwhelmed its handling capacity.

This prompted Postmaster General Lawrence O'Brien to recommend conversion of the Post Office Department to a government corporation. As O'Brien explained to President Lyndon Johnson, the new corporation would still be responsible to the federal government but would operate like an independent business. O'Brien expected that, as an independent business, the post office would operate more efficiently because it would have to pay for expenses with its own revenues instead of relying on government funding. In response, President Johnson appointed Frederick Kappel, retired board chairman of American Telephone and Telegraph, to head the new Commission on Postal Organization.

In June of 1968, the commission issued a report that agreed with O'Brien's recommendation to turn the Post Office Department into a government corporation and run it like an independent business. The report predicted that this change would improve the Post Office Department's services, equipment, and facilities, allowing it to become self-sustaining. It also stated that, although the new postal organization would report to the federal government, it should not receive federal subsidies. Not everyone in the post office and Congress favored these recommendations. However, the Postal Reorganization Act became law in August of 1970. And on July 1, 1971, the reorganized department officially began operating under its new name, the United States Postal Service.

The Postal Reorganization Act eliminated political patronage in appointments and promotions. It also protected the rights of employees to join (or not to join) labor organizations and gave these organizations the authority to bargain with management over wages. However, it prohibited strikes. And the act required postal employees' wages to be comparable to those offered by private businesses.

*The postmaster general and the board of governors operate out of the postal service's Washington, D.C., headquarters.*

# FOUR

# The Structure of Today's USPS

$A$ board of governors runs the USPS. With the advice and consent of the Senate, the president of the United States appoints the nine members of the board. They in turn select the postmaster general, who works with them to appoint the deputy postmaster general. These 11 people constitute the board of governors.

The USPS Board of Governors controls the organization's finances much as a corporate board does in the private sector. The USPS is supposed to finance its operation with postal revenues from the sale of stamps and other postal services. However, if the USPS loses money, it may borrow up to $10 billion from the general public. If necessary, the Treasury Department will pay postal debts.

The board of governors also controls the USPS's policies. As the chief executive officer, the postmaster general provides overall direction for the corporation. The deputy postmaster general directs postal operations and acts as liaison with the five regional

*In 1982, John R. McKean was appointed chairman of the USPS's board of governors.*

postmasters general. He and the postmaster general work in the USPS headquarters building in Washington, D.C., where various departments coordinate the functions of the field staff.

At the headquarters level, the associate postmaster general also reports to the postmaster general. He oversees the work of four major divisions: employee and labor relations, marketing and communications, facilities and supply, and management information and research technology. Like similar divisions in large private companies, each division develops policies for its part of the organization. A senior assistant postmaster general (SAPMG) manages each division. Within each division, an assistant postmaster general (APMG) manages one of several departments.

Three other divisions report directly to the postmaster general at the headquarters location. These divisions are headed by the chief inspector, the general counsel, and the SAPMG of finance and planning.

In the field, the USPS organization has five postal regions. A regional postmaster general manages the area's activities and is responsible for providing quality mail service in that area. He has complete authority over regional personnel and daily operations. Although he is the chief decision-maker for the area, the organization's decentralized structure permits his managers to make decisions, too.

Each region subdivides into sectional centers and then into individual post offices. Sectional centers are large facilities that handle all mail processing for a particular geographic area. Individual post offices bring mail to their area's sectional center, where the mail is postmarked, sorted, and then transported to post offices, airports, and sectional centers that are closer to the mail's destinations.

Another part of the USPS is an independent agency called the Postal Rate Commission. (Rate-setting is such a complex process and involves so many factors that the USPS must devote an entire department to the constant review and development of mail rates.) Created by the Postal Reorganization Act in 1970, the commission has five members, who are appointed by the president.

As a part of its responsibilities, the commission submits recommendations to the Board of Governors on postage rates and fees and on mail classification. It studies postal matters, such as costing theory and operations, and issues opinions on the effects of proposed changes in postal service. The commission receives, studies, and issues to the USPS recommendations and reports on complaints about postage rates, mail classifications, and postal services. Finally, it acts on appeals regarding the closing or consolidation of small post offices.

# The USPS Organization

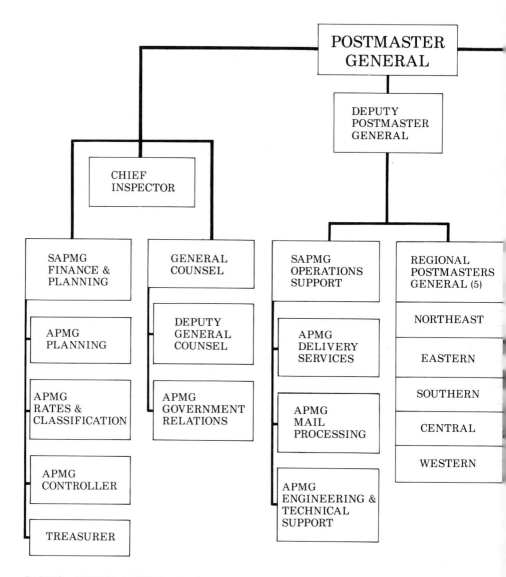

SAPMG—SENIOR ASSISTANT POSTMASTER GENERAL
APMG—ASSISTANT POSTMASTER GENERAL

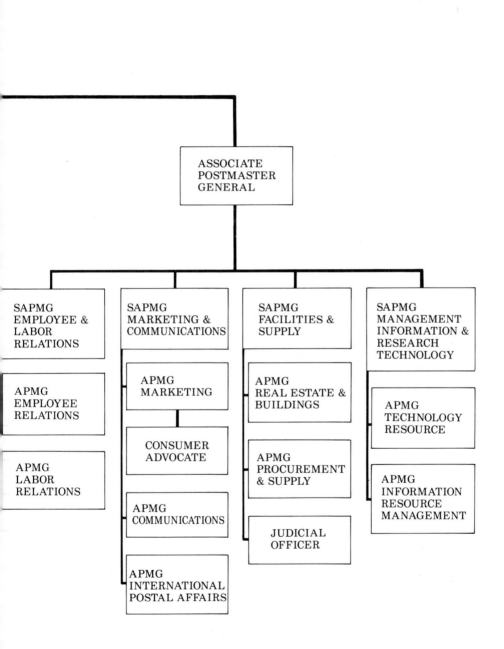

ASSOCIATE
POSTMASTER
GENERAL

SAPMG
EMPLOYEE &
LABOR
RELATIONS

APMG
EMPLOYEE
RELATIONS

APMG
LABOR
RELATIONS

SAPMG
MARKETING &
COMMUNICATIONS

APMG
MARKETING

CONSUMER
ADVOCATE

APMG
COMMUNICATIONS

APMG
INTERNATIONAL
POSTAL AFFAIRS

SAPMG
FACILITIES &
SUPPLY

APMG
REAL ESTATE &
BUILDINGS

APMG
PROCUREMENT
& SUPPLY

JUDICIAL
OFFICER

SAPMG
MANAGEMENT
INFORMATION &
RESEARCH
TECHNOLOGY

APMG
TECHNOLOGY
RESOURCE

APMG
INFORMATION
RESOURCE
MANAGEMENT

# United States Postal Service Regions ───────────

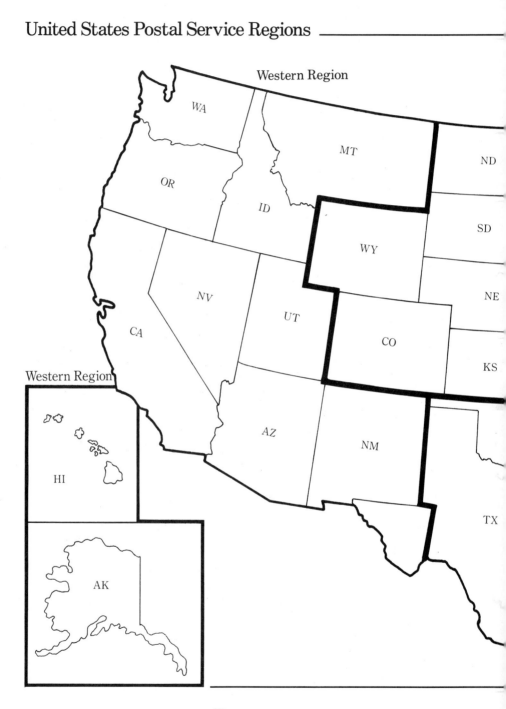

Central Region

Northeast Region

Eastern Region

Southern Region

MN
WI
MI
IA
IL
IN
OH
MO
KY
OK
AR
TN
MS
AL
GA
LA
FL
ME
VT
NH
NY
MA
CT
RI
PA
NJ
MD
DE
DC
WV
VA
NC
SC

*The USPS processes thousands of packages each day.*

# FIVE

# Moving the Mail

For the USPS, the process of mail handling begins when a postal customer mails a letter. If he wants to mail a first-class letter, he can do this by taking the letter to a post office, depositing it in a mail collection box, or leaving it in his personal mailbox.

If he chooses to mail the letter at a post office, he may need to think about the type of postal service he needs. For the complete range of mail services, he should visit one of the 30,000 full-service post offices. For most services, he can visit one of 9,000 postal branches, postal stations, or community post offices. But if he just needs to mail a letter or package, buy stamps, or use certain simple services, he can stop at one of the 1,300 self-service postal centers, which are open 24 hours a day.

If he chooses to drop his letter in a mail collection box, he can find out exactly when it will be collected by checking the daily pickup schedule on the box. Some mail collection boxes are designated for local mail only; others are marked for out-of-town

*Self-service post offices operate 24 hours a day.*

mail. In a city or town, these boxes are located on many street corners, in most large office buildings, and in some apartment complexes.

If the sender chooses to leave the letter in his mailbox, a letter carrier will collect it when he delivers the mail. Postal workers have to collect letters deposited anywhere other than in a post office and bring them to a nearby post office. Letter carriers usually collect letters and packages from mail collection boxes several times a day.

# Processing Letters

After the letter reaches the post office, a postal clerk puts it in a sack with hundreds of other letters. Then the letters travel by truck to a sectional center for processing. Sectional centers handle almost all of the incoming and outgoing mail for the post offices they serve. (Local post offices handle the mail going to addresses within their area, collected from "local" mail collection boxes.)

To sort large amounts of mail efficiently, sectional centers use high-speed, automated equipment. First, clerks empty the mail sacks onto conveyor belts that carry the mail to an edger-feeder. The edger-feeder sorts envelopes by size and feeds them into a facer-canceler, which faces them all in the same direction, cancels their stamps, and prints postmarks on them. Postmark information includes the date; the sectional center's name, state, and ZIP code; and the time period in which the post office received the letter.

Next, the letters travel to an optical character reader for further sorting. Optical character readers are computerized machines that "read" the ZIP codes on envelopes and move the envelopes to another machine that sprays them with marks that form bar codes. Then bar code sorters translate these marks and sort the letters by region. For mail traveling within the region, other bar code machines do two more sortings—once by destination post office and once by delivery route.

Mail that will travel outside of the region is bundled and put into mailbags. These bags are trucked to an airport for loading onto airplanes. From the destination airport, the mailbags travel

*Workers load loose mail onto conveyor belts for processing.*

*A worker places mail into a bar code sorter.*

by truck to a sectional center, where the mail is sorted according to ZIP code. Trucks then carry the mail to the destination post office.

The destination post office gives letter carriers the mail for places on their routes. The carriers then sort the mail in slotted cases arranged in the order of delivery. Although some letter carriers deliver mail by car or special USPS vehicle, many deliver the mail on foot. In most towns, the carrier uses his vehicle as a mini-warehouse. He loads all his deliveries into the car or truck, parks on each block on his route, and loads his bag with that block's mail for delivery on foot.

The USPS provides city, rural, and general delivery—three very different types of delivery. Towns with more than 2,500 people or 750 mail stops qualify for city delivery. However, these towns must provide paved roads, sidewalks, street signs, and house numbers. Rural areas that have passable roads throughout the year receive rural delivery, but each household must place a mailbox along the road. (People who live in areas with impassable roads must pick up their mail.) In most areas, an individual without a permanent address can qualify for general delivery. However, he must inform the post office in advance that he would like

74

his mail held until he picks it up.

Sometimes the mail can't be delivered, because the addressee has moved without leaving a forwarding address, for example. Then the mail is sent back to the return address. When mail can't be delivered and can't be returned to its sender (usually because the return address is unknown), it goes to the dead letter office. Sometimes the dead letter staff can find a return address or other helpful information inside the letter or package. If so, it sends the item to the address it finds. If it can't find any evidence about the sender or the addressee, the post office is permitted to keep any money it finds in the dead letters or gets from the sale of undeliverable packages.

## Processing Bulk Mail

For the processing of bulk mail—packages, magazines, advertisements, and other large-size mailings—the post office uses another method. Although the post office collects and delivers bulk mail the same way it does letter mail, it sorts and handles bulk mail differently.

Like letter mail, bulk mail is sent to a sectional center by local post offices. But unlike letter mail, once the bulk mail reaches the sectional center, it is bundled into sacks or containers and transported by truck to an automated bulk mail center or support center.

At the bulk mail center, conveyor belts move the mail sacks from postal trucks to machines that empty the sacks. To sort the mail, postal workers use computerized machines. After it is sorted, trucks and planes transport the bulk mail leaving the region. Bulk mail staying within the region is trucked to a sectional center for further sorting. Then it's sent to the destination post office, where it's sorted by delivery route. Finally, the employees at the destination post office deliver the packages and other bulk mail when they deliver letters.

*The U.S. Postal Service competes with independent couriers through innovative services such as Express Mail.*

# SIX

# A Look at Postal Services

The USPS offers a surprisingly wide variety of postal services that range from special delivery to the production and sale of collectible stamps. A common service that many people take for granted is mail delivery. The USPS has set up five classes of mail, each with its own postage rate and type of delivery service: express, first class, second class, third class, and fourth class.

Express is the fastest class of mail. It guarantees next-day mail delivery of letters and packages weighing less than 70 pounds (32 kilograms) to specified destination post offices. The post office has established an excellent record, delivering more than 120,000 express mail packages on time every day. Express mail is the most expensive class, but it offers the speed and convenience of overnight delivery and is competitive with private companies offering similar services.

First-class mail consists of letters, postcards, greeting cards, and many other types of material. It travels more quickly and

*Publishers bundle magazines for second-class mailing.*

costs more than all other classes of mail except express, and it can't be opened for inspection without a federal search warrant.

Second-class mail applies only to magazines and newspapers. Because the government pays for part of the cost of handling this class of mail, a publisher must request second-class mailing privileges from the government. Large volume helps keep second-class mail rates low.

Third-class mail, or bulk business mail, includes parcels and printed matter that weigh less than 16 ounces (443.2 grams). Usually, large mailers pay third-class rates to mail advertisements, catalogs, and small merchandise samples. Although third-class is more economical to use than first-class, mail takes longer to reach its destination.

Fourth-class mail, or parcel post, refers to packages that weigh 1 to 70 pounds (0.5 to 31.8 kilograms) and measure less than 108 inches (274.32 centimeters) in combined length and girth. Special fourth-class rates apply to such materials as books and catalogs. Fourth-class is less expensive than express mail service, but its delivery is not as fast.

The post office provides additional delivery services to those with special needs. Customers who require speedy delivery can request special delivery, priority mail, or special handling. Those who want their mail sent automatically to their new address can take advantage of mail forwarding, another special delivery service. Others may need to use the collect-on-delivery (COD) service, which allows them to order merchandise and pay for it when it's delivered.

## Electronic Mail Services

The USPS offers two high-speed electronic mail services: mailgrams and INTELPOST. Mailgram service provides next-day message delivery anywhere in the United States and Canada. A mailgram can be sent in one of two ways—by dictating a message to a Western Union telephone operator or by using an office Telex or teletypewriter exchange (TWX). Western Union transmits the message by telegraph to the destination post office. Then special machines receive and print the message, and a letter carrier delivers it with the regular mail.

For international electronic mail service, the USPS offers INTELPOST. To send an overnight message by INTELPOST, a machine called a facsimile reader must scan a document for transmission by satellite. In the destination country, a machine prints a black-and-white image of the document, which is then delivered by a local carrier.

## Other Postal Services

The post office offers customers services that protect the items they mail and give them proof of mailing or delivery. Each of these services—insurance, registered mail, certified mail, return receipts, and certificates of mailing—require an extra fee. For third- and fourth-class mail and packages sent by priority mail or first-class mail, insurance against loss or damage is available for the fair value of an item in amounts up to $500. For extremely valuable items sent by first class, registered mail allows the customer to purchase up to $25,000 of insurance. Certified mail, which is available only for first-class mail, provides proof of mailing and, if desired, a return receipt as proof of delivery. Return receipts can act as proof of delivery for mail that's insured for $25 or more as well as for express, COD, registered, and certified mail. A certificate of mailing simply gives a postal customer proof that he mailed a letter or package.

Perhaps the best-known postal service is the sale of stamps. Most postal customers buy stamps to use when mailing letters, but many others buy stamps for their collections. Stamp collecting, or philately, is the most popular hobby in the world. In the United States alone, about 20 million people are stamp collectors. Many of them visit the post office regularly to buy new or recently-issued stamps and postal stationery. To help these enthusiastic hobbyists, many post offices also sell stamp collecting kits, books, mint sets of commemorative and special stamps, and other philatelic products.

Currently, the post office sells five types of United States stamps. *Regular or definitive stamps* are printed in unlimited quantities and are the most common. *Commemorative stamps* are

**Insured mail protects valuable items from loss or damage. Certified mail provides a mailing receipt.**

*Millions of hobbyists around the world collect U.S. commemorative stamps, such as these honoring philately.*

large, colorful stamps—printed in limited numbers—that honor an important person, event, or subject. *Coil stamps* come in rolls, so each one has two perforated edges and two straight edges. *Airmail stamps* are available for sending mail overseas. *Postage due stamps* are used for mail that doesn't have enough postage.

Post offices offer their customers many other services. They sell money orders for up to $700, which provide a safe way to send money. They usually accept personal checks as payment for postal services and products. When requested, they give receipts for cash payments. Some post offices even accept passport applications. For a rental fee, many post offices offer the anonymity and convenience of post office (P.O.) boxes. The P.O. box number serves as the box renter's address, and he can pick up mail from his locked P.O. box any time the post office lobby is open. When boxes aren't available or customers expect large amounts of mail, they can request that mail be held for pickup during regular post office hours. This is known as caller, or pickup, service.

The post office also rents postage meters, which print the exact postage, postmark, and date on mail. Many businesspeople use these meters to save time. By preparing their own mail, they avoid waiting in post office lines while each piece is weighed, posted, and tallied for payment. The meter records and subtracts the amount of postage used from a prepaid postage allowance. When the meter indicates the allowance is running out, the renter takes the meter to the post office and pays to have it reset.

*Technological advances, such as the use of video cameras to monitor mail flow, keep the USPS competitive.*

# SEVEN

# Postal Plans
# for the Future

The Postal Reorganization Act completely changed the way the postal organization did business. Despite problems and adjustments in the first 15 years, the new USPS has earned a profit and increased its mail volume in 3 of the last 4 years. And it did this despite the loss of federal subsidies and the emergence of strong competition from new technologies and private express mail carriers, such as Federal Express.

In 1984 alone, 702,123 USPS employees moved 131.5 billion pieces of mail. Of these employees, 444,656 were mail handlers, clerks, carriers, or drivers. The others provided supervision, direction, and technical assistance as postmasters, supervisors, maintenance workers, postal inspectors, or managers.

The future role of the USPS will depend heavily on the role society wants—or needs—it to play. In colonial days, the goal of the postal service was to make money. Later, during the fledgling years of the United States, the main objective was to ensure communication between the states, not to make a profit.

*Flat sorting machines and other equipment speed mail sorting and delivery.*

Changes in society and technology affect people's expectations of the postal service. Years ago, many believed that all rates should be the same and that everyone should have speedy mail delivery. At the time, the post office could meet these goals, partly because of its federal subsidies and partly because of its monopoly on letter mail.

But times have changed. The Postal Reorganization Act modified the department's monopoly by allowing private carriers to deliver "extremely urgent" mail. With other companies competing for postal business, the USPS will need to offer more and better services at competitive prices.

In several areas, the USPS has already begun to improve its services. It has upgraded existing post office lobbies and has designed new lobbies to improve traffic flow and make the environment more attractive. At some post office windows, the USPS has begun to install computerized terminals. This should provide fast access to rate and service information and reduce customer waiting time in lobbies. Some offices are trying to speed service with the "lobby sweep" program, in which a postal supervisor is stationed in the lobby to give information and forms to waiting customers. The USPS also speeds service by placing self-service stamp machines in most post office lobbies and offering stamps-by-mail.

The Postal Reorganization Act also ended the department's reliance on subsidies. This forces the USPS to work harder at controlling its costs. For instance, it has to work closely with the postal unions to reduce overtime and other employee expenses while continuing to pay competitive salaries. To save money on delivery, the USPS is testing and may eventually use vehicles with much longer life expectancies.

The USPS also is beginning to rely on postal customers to help reduce costs. For large volume customers, the USPS already offers postage discounts on mail that's presorted by ZIP

*Computerized scales help clerks handle customers faster.*

*Locked postal boxes at centralized locations are convenient for both mail carriers and their customers.*

code. The customer saves money and so does the postal service, because presorting reduces USPS handling costs. For individual customers, the USPS hopes to increase the use of P.O. boxes as well as neighborhood delivery and collection boxes. These boxes save on delivery costs and give customers the safety of locked letter-boxes.

So much mail travels by air that the USPS will need to find ways to control air transport costs. Airline deregulation has made this difficult, but the USPS has begun to study the problems involved in air transport and will probably change the way it awards air contracts.

The USPS has already begun to feel the effects of new technologies such as communications devices, computers, and satellites. For a long time, it had focused its energies on letter and parcel mail. But recently, the USPS began to dedicate more time and resources to investigating new technologies. It is expanding its INTELPOST network and continuing to experiment with other innovations, but it will still have to face intense competition from other companies entering the new communications markets.

Technological advances should help the USPS become more efficient. As researchers develop devices such as wand readers, laser scanners, and more advanced optical character readers, the postal service will test them to see how well they can improve mail processing.

The American postal service has evolved along with the nation, from the colonial days to the age of communication. It has weathered many hardships and survived a major reorganization. The USPS will continue to change as the nation's needs change and grow as it grows.

# GLOSSARY

Airmail—Mail that is transported by jet or airplane.

Bar code—A sorting code that can be read by a machine called a bar code sorter.

Dead letter office—A central office that handles undeliverable and unreturnable mail.

Edger-feeder—A machine that sorts mail by size and feeds it into a facer-canceler.

Facer-canceler—A machine that faces all envelopes in one direction, cancels stamps, and prints postmarks.

Mochila—A leather saddle cover with a small, locked mail pouch used by pony express riders.

Optical character reader—A machine that can "read" an address.

Parcel post—Package delivery service.

Philately—The hobby of stamp collecting.

Post road—A route over which the post office carries mail.

Postrider—A person who carried mail on horseback between post offices.

Rural free delivery (RFD)—Free mail delivery to residents of small towns, farm communities, and other isolated areas.

ZIP code—A five-digit number, or zone improvement plan code, that helps route mail correctly and efficiently.

# SELECTED REFERENCES

Clinton, Alan. *The Post Office Worker: A Trade Union and Social History.* Boston: Allen Unwin, Inc., 1984.

Cullinan, Gerald. *The United States Postal Service.* New York: Praeger Pubs., 1973.

Feldman, Helen B. *The American Postal Service from the Beginning to 1710.* New York: Brooklyn College Press, 1939.

Fleishman, Joel L. *The Future of the Postal Service.* New York: Praeger Pubs., 1983.

Fuller, Wayne F. *The American Mail: Enlarger of the Common Life.* Chicago: University of Chicago Press, 1980.

Margolis, Richard J. *At the Crossroads, An Inquiry into Rural Post Offices and the Communities They Serve.* Government Printing Office, 1980.

Scheele, Carl H. *A Short History of the Mail Service.* Washington: Smithsonian Institute Press, 1970.

Sherwin, Roger, ed. *Perspectives on Postal Issues.* Washington: American Enterprise Institute for Public Policy Research, 1980.

Tierney, John T. *Postal Reorganization: Managing the Public's Business.* Dover, Mass.: Auburn House Publishing Co., Inc., 1981.

---

**ACKNOWLEDGMENTS**

The author and publishers are grateful to these organizations for information and photographs: H. Armstrong Roberts; Library of Congress; Maryland Historical Society, Baltimore; National Archives and Records Administration; Smithsonian Institution, Washington, D.C.; United States Postal Service. Picture Research: Imagefinders, Inc.

# INDEX

## A
Airline Deregulation Act of 1978 49

airmail 44–49, 87

American Postal Machine Company 55

American Revolution 25, 27, 28

American Telephone and Telegraph 55

APMG (Assistant Postmaster General) 64, 66–67

Armstrong, George B. 37

Army Signal Corps 46

automation 55–59

## B
Bache, Richard 26

Baltimore 25, 40, 43

Barry, William T. 29

Benger, Elliot 24

Board of Governors 63, 65

Boyle, George L. 46

British Post Office, American Branch 24

Bryce, James 9

bulk mail 75, 78

business 11, 13, 14

Butterfield, John 33

## C
cabinet 9, 11

California 32, 34

*California, The* 33

Canada 24, 79

Carson, Kit 33

certificate of mailing 79

certified mail 79

Chicago 37, 38, 48, 59

Chicago and Northwestern Railroad 37

Civil Aeronautics Board 49

coast-to-coast service 33, 39, 47

COD (collect-on-delivery) 79, 80

collection 71, 72

colonies 21–25

Colorado 34

Commission on Postal Organization 60

communication 17–19

Congress 27, 28, 32, 36, 52–55

Constitution 28

constitutional post office 25

Continental Congress 26

Curtis, George William 9

## D
Davis, William A. 37

dead letter office 75

delivery 74, 75

Department of Commerce 49

Department of State 8

Department of the Treasury 8, 28, 29, 50, 51, 63

Department of War 8

Depression 11, 42, 57

Downing, William 39

## E
electronic mail 79

England 22, 23, 25

executive branch 8, 9, 11

express mail 77, 78

## F
Fast Mail 38, 39

Federal Express 83

Federal Highway Act 53

*Federalist Papers, The* 7

finances 50, 60, 61, 63, 84–86

first-class mail 77, 79

Florida 21, 24

Ford, Henry 40